*Alexandra
let's fight hate
together
love you
Alex*

Fig

How to Win Others with Love

By

Serge Destin

ISBN: 9781692094461

Imprint: Independently published October, 2019

Printed in United States of America

Kindle Independent Publishing

Dedication

I thank God for choosing me, an unworthy servant saved by grace, to contribute to His work.

I dedicate this book to you. The fact that you are holding this publication shows that you are a FIGHTER. We are caught in a struggle between good and evil, righteousness and sin, love and hate. You and I need to keep fighting; WE WILL WIN.

Table of Contents

Introduction

Why is there so much hate in this world, even among Christians? The history of Christianity is marred by dark periods: persecutions, wars, crusades, slavery, and racism. Christianity more than any other institutions has been blamed for the woes of the world today. The unfortunate reality is that it is true. No wonder the famous Beatles singer, John Lennon, wrote these words in his song IMAGINE

Imagine there's no heaven

It's easy if you try

No hell below us

Above us only sky

Imagine all the people

Living for today

Imagine there's no countries

It isn't hard to do

Nothing to kill or die for

And no religion, too

The underlying reason is that Christians don't love like Jesus did anymore. Jesus' life was a blueprint for living, loving, and treating others. The first generation of Christians followed in the footsteps of the Master. However, the church took a turn for the worst at the beginning of the 4th Century A.D. Ever since, it found itself in a downward spiral going further and further away from the teachings of Jesus Christ.

A few of years ago, I decided to read the entire Bible. It took me about two years and a half to complete this feat. During that time, my mind expanded; I gained a greater knowledge of God and His Word. Most importantly, I gained a deeper understanding of His Love and the first epistle of John was an eye-opener. This epistle focused essentially on the Love of God for us, and how we should love others in return. It blew me away.

The sad part about this experience is that the love that is taught in most Christian churches today doesn't come close to what John was teaching in his days. No wonder Christian believers all over the world are constantly complaining of the lack of love in their congregation. As a Christian from birth and a repeat victim of Christian malice and hatred, I got to see up close the difference between the life of the Savior and those who claim to love and follow Him. And what a difference it is!

I am not blaming Christian leaders because I know why they don't talk about love the way the apostle did; the reason is what is required is very hard for any human, including myself, to practice. Loving like Jesus did is tough as you will discover while reading this book, yet beautiful and amazing.

In the epistle of 1 John, the apostle made a call to his readers to love not like the world. The book that you are holding in your hands is largely on this epistle and reiterates the call that the apostle made. It expounds on the principles of love Jesus lived by. If you don't understand and apply them in your life, you will become a lifeless Christian, a hypocrite, and a fraud.

So, don't delay in reading this book; let's FIGHT HATE in our heart and in the society at large. I promise that you will have a new appreciation for Jesus and for the people around you. After all, isn't your goal to spread LOVE and be an agent of PEACE wherever you go?

I hope that through the reading of this book you will have a better understanding of the love of God and how to love others in return.

Chapter 1

Sons and Daughters of God

In Genesis chapter 1 & 2, the Bible presents the creation of the world in Seven days. Although there are many aspects of creation that I don't really understand, I believe it's true. I know that sounds dogmatic, but the reality is that there are many things you and I believe in that we don't understand, such as gravity. We know that it is the force that prevents us from floating all over the place, aside from that we don't understand much about it. We can't touch it, feel it, nor see it. Yet, we don't question its existence.

Also, love is a concept that we poorly understand. However, the whole world believes that love exists. People sing about it every day. Most movies include some kind of love story or scene. Millions of sermons and presentations are given all over the world in different settings trying to explain it. Yet, it remains one of the biggest mysteries of our world, an elusive idea that billions of people on this planet are searching for.

Yes, I believe in creation. I will not take the time to explain evolution which is a theory that I am familiar with because that would be a total waste of time in the context of this book. According to Genesis, men and women are from noble origins.

[26] And God said, Let us make man in our image, after our likeness: and let them have dominion over the fish of the sea, and over the fowl of the air, and over the cattle, and over all the earth, and over every creeping thing that creepeth upon the earth.

[27] So God created man in his own image, in the image of God created he him; male and female created he them.

[28] And God blessed them, and God said unto them, Be fruitful, and multiply, and replenish the earth, and subdue it: and have dominion over the fish of the sea,

and over the fowl of the air, and over every living thing that moveth upon the earth.

Genesis 1: 26- 28

[7] And the Lord God formed man of the dust of the ground, and breathed into his nostrils the breath of life; and man became a living soul.

[8] And the Lord God planted a garden eastward in Eden; and there he put the man whom he had formed.

Genesis 2: 7- 8

[20] And Adam gave names to all cattle, and to the fowl of the air, and to every beast of the field; but for Adam there was not found an help meet for him.

[21] And the Lord God caused a deep sleep to fall upon Adam, and he slept: and he took one of his ribs, and closed up the flesh instead thereof;

[22] And the rib, which the Lord God had taken from man, made he a woman, and brought her unto the man.

23 And Adam said, This is now bone of my bones, and flesh of my flesh: she shall be called Woman, because she was taken out of Man.

24 Therefore shall a man leave his father and his mother, and shall cleave unto his wife: and they shall be one flesh.

25 And they were both naked, the man and his wife, and were not ashamed.

Genesis 2:20- 25

Humanity was created by God; more importantly men and women were made in the image of the Creator. What a great honor to be made in the likeness of God instead of coming out of apes. How uplifting is it to know that we are not random acts of nature, purposeless beings who came into existence by chance, but instead our existence had been planned. You and I are here because we are supposed to be, the universe would be missing out if you weren't born. You may not know yet what your specific purpose is and what role you must play, but if you keep searching in the right direction, using the Bible as your guide, you will figure it out.

Adam and Eve were happy; they were living in paradise. They lacked nothing, plenty of beautiful, flavorful, and healthy food. Work was light. There were no diseases, no worries, no insecurities, and no death. What else could they ask for? There was only one simple and clear restriction and they decided to violate it and lose everything they had.

By their disobedience, they introduced sin into the world. Many religions define "sin" differently thus, making it a relative term. However, the Bible gives a clear definition:

Whosoever committeth sin transgresseth also the law: for sin is the transgression of the law. 1 John 3: 4

The Bible defines it as the violation of the law of God. Adam and Eve were told in the Garden of Eden not to eat the fruits of a very specific tree that is referred to as the "tree of knowledge of good and evil."

16 And the Lord God commanded the man, saying, Of every tree of the garden thou mayest freely eat:

17 But of the tree of the knowledge of good and evil, thou shalt not eat of it: for in the day that thou eatest thereof thou shalt surely die.

Genesis 2: 16- 17

They disobeyed that one simple law even though they knew that the consequences would be disastrous -read Genesis 3 if you are not familiar with the story. Life as they knew it came to an end the moment they ate the fruit. They started seeing death everywhere in the leaves of the trees as well as in the animal kingdom. They experienced diseases, pain, fear, and insecurities. Their view of themselves changed completely; they were ashamed. Furthermore, the way they appreciated and loved each other changed as well:

- In Genesis 2, Adam was sad to be alone. In chapter 3, he was ready to put Eve on the chopping block.

- Prior to sin, he saw her as a "help meet," after sin, he considered her as the source of his trouble.

- When they met, Adam called her "flesh of MY flesh and bone of MY bone," after he ate the forbidden fruit, he referred to her as "THE woman thou gavest me."

Sin didn't just bring sufferings and death into this world, but its greatest effect was destroying love between God and His creatures and love between humans.

I want to clarify that God's love for us hasn't change, which I'll explore with you in later chapters. However, our love for Him has decreased drastically, which in turn makes it very difficult for us to understand His love for us.

From Adam and Eve, two opposing groups of people emerged: Cain, who represented those who were rebellious toward God versus Abel and Seth, who represented those who served God. From that time, people who chose to love God are referred to as the Sons of God.

That the sons of God saw the daughters of men that they were fair; and they took them wives of all which they chose. Genesis 6: 2.

Behold, what manner of love the Father hath bestowed upon us, that we should be called the sons of God: therefore the world knoweth us not, because it knew him not.

[2] Beloved, now are we the sons of God, and it doth not yet appear what we shall be: but we know that, when he

shall appear, we shall be like him; for we shall see him as he is.

[3] And every man that hath this hope in him purifieth himself, even as he is pure.

1 John 3:1- 3

Therefore, being a son or daughter of God is a choice that you and I have to make. If we choose to be on the side of God, we will have to go through a purifying process that Christians typically referred to as the NEW BIRTH. Apostle John introduced us to this concept when he related the words of Jesus to Nicodemus:

There was a man of the Pharisees, named Nicodemus, a ruler of the Jews:

[2] The same came to Jesus by night, and said unto him, Rabbi, we know that thou art a teacher come from God: for no man can do these miracles that thou doest, except God be with him.

Serge Destin

³ Jesus answered and said unto him, Verily, verily, I say unto thee, Except a man be born again, he cannot see the kingdom of God.

⁴ Nicodemus saith unto him, How can a man be born when he is old? can he enter the second time into his mother's womb, and be born?

⁵ Jesus answered, Verily, verily, I say unto thee, Except a man be born of water and of the Spirit, he cannot enter into the kingdom of God.

⁶ That which is born of the flesh is flesh; and that which is born of the Spirit is spirit.

⁷ Marvel not that I said unto thee, Ye must be born again.

John 3:1-7

Those who choose to be sons or daughters of God and go through the new birth experience will avoid the impurities of sins and uphold the commandments of God.

Now, let's look at the other camp, those who don't want to submit to the Creator by answering this question: What are the characteristics that show that someone is not a child of God?

[10] In this the children of God are manifest, and the children of the devil: whosoever doeth not righteousness is not of God, neither he that loveth not his brother. 1 John 3:10.

Many people are disappointed by those who called themselves CHRISTIANS. They look at what is happening in Christian churches today, at the behaviors of church leaders, and at the coldness and judgmental attitudes of the members and decide to turn their back on Christ. Let me share a little secret with you. Anybody can claim the name of Jesus, anybody can join a Christian denomination, and anybody can register as a church member, however that doesn't mean that he or she is accepted by God as His son or daughter.

In the verse above, John gave two important characteristics of those who are not children of God, aka sons of the devil. The first one is "Whoever does not practice righteousness" (NKJV). Righteousness has to do with people doing what is right. The question you are probably asking yourself is "How do I know what is right?" In this society "the right thing" is a relative term. I am sure you have heard somebody saying in an argument "what's right for you, is not necessarily right for me." Maybe you've used this saying to defend your position on a specific issue. Therefore, you and I cannot rely on our own interpretation of what's right to deem somebody righteous or not. Somebody may seem to be a good and nice person by my own standards, while being judged as a bad and evil human being by somebody else's yardstick. For instance, some Americans believe that the current president of the United States of America is a brilliant politician and is the right man for our time; while others see him as a dishonest businessman who should be removed from office. The point is if we want to determine whether someone is a righteous person in an absolute non-bias way, we need to have an absolute un-bias standard. The Bible solves that issue for us as God gave us His standards called the TEN COMMANDMENTS found in Exodus 20: 2- 17. I will dive more into them in the next chapter.

The second characteristic is "He who does not love his brother" (NKJV). Someone who doesn't have love in his or her heart is not considered by God as His child even though he or she professes to serve Him. Over the years, I have seen and heard several preachers presenting messages of hate, discrimination, and violence under the guise of Christianity. They use the Bible to incite specific groups of people to molest certain type of individual just like the Word was used in the past to justify slavery. This is why I think it's very important for you to understand the fact that someone holds many titles such as bishop, pastor, prophet of Christ, or that he or she is popular, has his or her own TV show doesn't mean that he or she is   accepted in the family of God. Therefore, if a Christian, regardless of whether he or she is a leader or simple church member, doesn't show love to others or takes pleasure in performing unrighteous acts, he or she is considered a child of the devil. I know these are strong word; however, they are not meant to be judgmental but instead are filled with hope as you will discover in the following chapters.

Chapter 2

The Law of Love

Wherever there are two people or more assembled, there must be laws that regulate their behaviors, otherwise they won't be able to stand each other for a long period of time. Countries have laws that they abide to, so do schools, restaurants, and transportation. Furthermore, everybody who is part of a group must strictly abide by the rules in place otherwise the group's subsistence may be in question. Let's for instance consider the smallest unit of the society, a couple. Even though, they are two grown adults, there are rules that regulate the relationships between a husband and wife. For instance, if one of the spouses decides to have sex with someone else, then he or she breaks the law and put the marriage in jeopardy.

I hope that you realize how important and indispensable laws are. For these reasons, some groups select people to enforce them and punish those who violate them, for instance police officers and IRS agents. A variety of punishments can be applied upon those found guilty of transgressing them ranging from paying some fees, be imprisoned or expulsed, to even being put to death. This is a very serious matter that cannot be taken lightly.

Therefore, you can understand that laws cannot be random, and they cannot be left up to chance. They must be well thought of and studied with the utmost scrutiny. That's why in democratic societies, some of the brightest minds of the land, senators and congressmen/women, are selected to continually create new laws and revise the old ones. These processes are usually a long and strenuous.

It's no wonder that when God created Adam and Eve, He established some rules of conduct to regulate their behaviors and ensure their prosperity. For instance, they were supposed to cultivate and guard the garden of Eden, but not to cut the trees and destroy the environment. They were instructed to take care of the animals, but not to kill them to eat. The one negative rule that God gave them is to not eat the fruits of the tree of knowledge of good and evil.

[16] And the Lord God commanded the man, saying, Of every tree of the garden thou mayest freely eat:

[17] But of the tree of the knowledge of good and evil, thou shalt not eat of it: for in the day that thou eatest thereof thou shalt surely die.

Genesis 2: 16- 17

It's worth quoting this text again so I can break it down a little bit more. Let me point out a few words:

GOD COMMANDED: As Creator, He has the right to tell humans what to do and what not to do on Earth. It's a concept that's poorly understood, as many people question "Why didn't God want the first pair to eat of the tree of knowledge of good and evil?" The answer is simply BECAUSE HE DIDN'T WANT THEM TO. Remember the garden of Eden belongs to God, as such

He has the right to set rules for His guests, Adam and Eve. If a friend comes to spend a few days at your house, do you have the right to tell him that some rooms are off limit? Of course, you do. Do you have to tell him why? No, you don't owe him any explanation. It's your house; and your friend is obliged to abide by your rules as long as he is there, otherwise you have the right to ask him to leave.

God didn't tell why they couldn't eat of the fruit of that tree, but today we know that it was to test their allegiance and trust.

[4] Then the serpent said to the woman, "You will not surely die. [5] For God knows that in the day you eat of it your eyes will be opened, and you will be like God, knowing good and evil." Genesis 3: 4 -5.

By contradicting God, the serpent implied that the Creator was a liar and couldn't be trusted as such. He also put in Eve's mind the idea of becoming a goddess, being that she would not need God anymore and could potentially get rid of Him -This idea is still prevalent today. By eating the forbidden fruit, the first pair showed that they trusted the serpent rather than God.

THOU SHALT SURELY DIE: God warned them of the consequence of disobeying Him. Some people think that this was too harsh of a punishment for such a trivial act, in order words, the punishment didn't fit the crime. God is the source and sustainer of life, "[7] And the Lord God formed man *of* the dust of the ground, and breathed into his nostrils the breath of life; and man became a living being." Genesis 2: 7. As human, we need to be connected to God in order to live; just like the TV set must be connected to the power outlet to turn on. When it is unplugged, it is just a useless piece of equipment in the living room. Check out the reaction of Adam and Eve toward God after they disobeyed,

[8] And they heard the sound of the Lord God walking in the garden in the cool of the day, and Adam and his

wife hid themselves from the presence of the Lord God among the trees of the garden.

9 Then the Lord God called to Adam and said to him, "Where *are* you?"

10 So he said, "I heard Your voice in the garden, and I was afraid because I was naked; and I hid myself."

Genesis 3: 8-10.

They hid themselves; they disconnected themselves from God, the sustainer of their lives. Death is not a punishment, but the outcome of a life separated from the Life Giver. Furthermore, God was not the one who chose to separate Himself from them, they made that choice themselves.

The Old Commandments

After the fall, those who chose to follow God continued to obey His laws. The Bible doesn't give much detail as to what they were, but we know so well that there were some commandments in place.

[4] And I will make your descendants multiply as the stars of heaven; I will give to your descendants all these lands; and in your seed all the nations of the earth shall be blessed; [5] because Abraham obeyed My voice and kept My charge, My commandments, My statutes, and My laws." Genesis 26: 4- 6.

It seems like they were orally transmitted up to the time God gave Moses the Ten Commandments on Mount Sinai (Exodus 20: 2- 17). Let's take a quick look at each one of them. When studying them I like to look at them in reverse order, it's just my thing. At the end of each command ask yourself, "Is this a good law?"

COMMANDMENT #10: [17] "You shall not covet your neighbor's house; you shall not covet your neighbor's wife, nor his male servant, nor his female servant, nor his ox, nor his donkey, nor anything that *is* your neighbor's." A synonym for covet is to envy. Do you envy other people's stuff? Do you like it when other people envy your possessions? Envy gives rise to some of the worst crimes committed on earth. How many people have been killed just because they have a nice car or house that the murderer wanted for him or herself? How many jewelry stores, banks, or malls have been robbed because the thieves desired the goods, but weren't willing to do the work necessary to obtain them legally. So, is this a good law?

COMMANDMENT #9: [16] "You shall not bear false witness against your neighbor." One day someone called my workplace; the call was transferred to me since I was the supervisor. The person at the other end of the line asked to speak to Jane Doe; she wasn't working that day. Then he proceeded to tell me that, "I need to speak to her because I usually meet with her at the entry (in front of the building where I work) to smoke marijuana. She usually sells me some too." The next day, when I met Jane, I recounted to her the strange call I got. She told me that sounded like the kind of story her ex-boyfriend would make up to get her in trouble. In our society, telling unverified and unsubstantiated stories about others have become the norm. Some people make a fortune by gossiping on TV or in magazines. Would you like someone to make up stories about you? Is this a good law?

COMMANDMENT #8: [15] "You shall not steal." On December 11, 2008, Bernard Lawrence Madoff aka Bernie Madoff was arrested; the Americans were shocked as the news broke out. Bernie Madoff was up to that day one of the most respected financial advisor and financier in the country. He boasted an impressive resume which included former non-executive chairman of the NASDAQ Stock Market and chairman of Bernard L. Madoff Investment Securities. His firm was one of the tops in the financial industry until it was discovered it was a scam. Mr. Madoff perpetrated the largest Ponzi scheme in U.S. history defrauding over 4,800 clients of an estimated $ 64.8 billion. He is now serving a 150-year prison sentence. Would you like to be robbed of your life saving? Your car? Your identity? Honesty and integrity are rare qualities today unfortunately. Is this a good law?

COMMANDMENT #7: [14] "You shall not commit adultery." One of the biggest scandals to rock the political world was the Clinton-Lewinsky Affair. President Bill Clinton admitted to having, in his own words, an "inappropriate relationship" with a young White House intern name Monica Lewinsky. The country was divided as one group considered him guilty and was petitioning for his impeachment, while the other one saw the President as victim of a plot to get him out of office. Monica Lewinsky claimed to be a victim and that her reputation was damaged. The President almost lost his seat and his family; both parties lost. Adultery has destroyed many homes, ruined the lives of countless children, and has led many individuals to substance abuse, mental illnesses, suicide, and even to commit murder. Would you be hurt if you discover that your spouse or partner is cheating on you? Is this a good law?

COMMANDMENT #6: [13] "You shall not murder" (NKJV). When I saw this report in the news, I couldn't believe it. The anchor who was reporting the news couldn't believe it either. In 2012, a fight broke off between two men in Detroit; nobody was killed but two bystanders sustained minor injuries. The reason for the fight was KOOL-AID. Yes, you read it right. The men were arguing over who made the best KOOL-AID. The discussion escalated; they pulled out their guns and shot at each other. What a sad world we are living in today! A world where someone would attempt to kill another one over KOOL-AID. The value of human life is decreasing on a daily basis. People are being murdered every hour of the day; even innocent children are not spared. I hope you will never have a gun pointed at you or a member of your family. Is this a good law?

COMMANDMENT #5: [12] "Honor your father and your mother, that your days may be long upon the land which the Lord your God is giving you." I saw a video of a daughter beating her mother in a bus while cursing at her and calling her all kind of name. The mother looked old, tired, powerless, and defenseless. She didn't have the strength to tell her to stop. It was disheartening. Fortunately, a few passengers intervened otherwise the poor mother would have ended up in the hospital, maybe at the morgue. Love and respect between parents and children have reached a low point. I hope your kids, if you have any, respect and honor you. Is this a good law?

COMMANDMENT #3: [7] "You shall not take the name of the Lord your God in vain, for the Lord will not hold *him* guiltless who takes His name in vain." Members of any religion consider the name of their gods as sacred. No other god is attacked, mocked, and discredited as much as the God of the Bible and His Son Jesus-Christ. Look at the marvelous things He has done in your life, doesn't He deserve your respect and admiration. Is this a good law?

COMMANDMENT #2: [4]"You shall not make for yourself a carved image—any likeness *of anything* that *is* in heaven above, or that *is* in the earth beneath, or that *is* in the water under the earth; [5]you shall not bow down to them nor serve them. For I, the Lord your God, *am* a jealous God, visiting the iniquity of the fathers upon the children to the third and fourth *generations* of those who hate Me, [6]but showing mercy to thousands, to those who love Me and keep My commandments." The Bible states that God made man in His image using dust of the earth. Today, the great majority of men worship gods that they made from clay, gold, and wood. I don't know who the original author is, but I heard somebody say, "God created us in His image, we returned Him the favor." Forget the crucifix, the baby Jesus statue, or the Madonna; you don't need to bow before any sacred object of animal or human. Only, come to God in prayer; he is ready to hear you. Is this a good law?

COMMANDMENT #1: [2] "I *am* the Lord your God, who brought you out of the land of Egypt, out of the house of bondage.

[3] "You shall have no other gods before Me." Most religions aside from the Abrahamic ones, Judaism, Christianity, and Islam, are polytheistic, which means that they have many gods. God introduced Himself to the Israelites as the All-Powerful God, the One who did for them what no other gods could do, brought them out of Egypt. The ten plagues that were poured out on the Egyptians (Exodus 7- 12) and the crossing of the Red Sea (Exodus 14) were to prove to Israel, the Egyptians, and all the nations of the world that all the gods combine could not rival Him. Therefore, there is no reason to go after any of them. Serving Jehovah alone is enough. Is this a good law?

I am sure that you must have noticed that I skipped commandment #4. That's because this one holds a special place among the others. It is not superior nor more important, it's just different. Unfortunately, I will not spend time explaining it because many authors have done a wonderful job presenting it. I'll just list a few books as references:

- National Sunday Law by Jan Marcussen

- How to Keep the Sabbath Holy by Doug Batchelor

- Ten Commandments Twice Removed by Danny Shelton and Shelley Quinn

There is one aspect of this law that I want to point out though:

COMMANDMENT # 4: [8] Remember the sabbath day, to keep it holy.

[9] Six days shalt thou labour, and do all thy work:

[10] But the seventh day is the sabbath of the Lord thy God: in it thou shalt not do any work, thou, nor thy son, nor

thy daughter, thy manservant, nor thy maidservant, nor thy cattle, nor thy stranger that is within thy gates:

[11] For in six days the Lord made heaven and earth, the sea, and all that in them is, and rested the seventh day: wherefore the Lord blessed the sabbath day, and hallowed it.

The Sabbath was established since creation on the seventh day.

[1]Thus the heavens and the earth were finished, and all the host of them.

[2] And on the seventh day God ended his work which he had made; and he rested on the seventh day from all his work which he had made.

[3] And God blessed the seventh day, and sanctified it: because that in it he had rested from all his work which God created and made. Genesis 2: 1-3.

Adam and Eve kept this commandment while still in the garden of Eden. Therefore, the 4th commandment is a reminder of a principle that was forgotten by many after sin entered the world, hence the word "Remember" at the beginning of the command.

However at Sinai, the Sabbath commandment took on an additional function: it became the sign of those who recognize God as the Creator and want to serve Him alone. It is the proof of allegiance to Jehovah. It is not surprising that Jesus kept this commandment (Marc 1: 21; Marc 6: 2; Luke 4: 16, 31; Luke 13: 10) as well as the disciples (Acts 13: 14-15, 42- 44; Acts 17: 2). As a matter of fact, it is not until year 321 A.D. that Christians started accepting Sunday as a day of worship instead of Saturday to accommodate the pagans who were already used to worshiping the Sun-god on the first day of the week.

Therefore, keeping the Sabbath on the seventh day of the week, means that you are loyal to God, your Creator and Life-Giver, and to His Word. Is this a good law?

The New Commandments

You have probably noticed that the majority of Christians today don't keep the Ten Commandments; some reject them saying, "they were for the Jews," while others pick and choose which one to observe. However, one thing they all agree on is that Jesus gave these Two New Commandments:

[36] Master, which is the great commandment in the law?

[37] Jesus said unto him, Thou shalt love the Lord thy God with all thy heart, and with all thy soul, and with all thy mind.

[38] This is the first and great commandment.

[39] And the second is like unto it, Thou shalt love thy neighbour as thyself.

[40] On these two commandments hang all the law and the prophets.

Matthew 22: 36- 40

Love is the Great command that Jesus gave His followers; and you and I must learn to keep these two. However, are they really NEW? Was Christ the one who introduced the concept of love to the servant of Jehovah?

The truth is Jesus was only quoting what was already written. As a matter of fact, Moses, the one who presented the Ten Commandments to Israel, was the inspired author of the two so called NEW Commandments. Check it out:

And thou shalt love the Lord thy God with all thine heart, and with all thy soul, and with all thy might. Deuteronomy 6:5

Thou shalt not avenge, nor bear any grudge against the children of thy people, but thou shalt love thy neighbour as thyself: I am the Lord. Leviticus 19: 18

But the stranger that dwelleth with you shall be unto you as one born among you, and thou shalt love him as thyself; for ye were strangers in the land of Egypt: I am the Lord your God. Leviticus 19:34.

You see, Jesus didn't introduce NEW commandments; as a matter of fact, He didn't bring any NEW teachings during His earthly ministry, He only reinforced the old ones.

Furthermore, Jesus concluded His answer with these words, "On these two commandments hang all the law and the prophets." Matthew 22:40. In order words, these two are the foundation of the ten. If you look closely, you will see that commandment #1-4 talks about our love for God. If we love God, would we worship another one? If we love God, would we take His name in vain?

In addition, commandment #5-10 shows us how to love others starting with the ones closest to our hearts. If we love our parents, would we honor them? If we love our spouse, would we be faithful to him or her? Would we kill someone we love? You get the idea.

We cannot talk about love while rejecting the Commandments of God. It's impossible; they are forever intertwined. That's why when reading the book of 1 John, the author constantly refers to the Law of God.

Chapter 3

From Hate to Murder

I was talking to a coworker once and she was sharing with me the hardship she was going through. Most of her troubles were coming from her own family members. She blamed them for all kinds of trials. I could feel the bitterness and anger in her voice, so I asked her if she hated them. Her answer was, "I don't hate them; I just wish bad things happen to them." The word hate is usually considered to be the opposite of love. The Merriam-Webster dictionary defines it as an "Intense hostility and aversion usually deriving from fear, anger, or sense of injury; extreme dislike or disgust." It is not a good feeling to have. Unfortunately, it is extremely prevalent in our world today. Almost everyone living on this earth has at some point in his or her life hated or was hated by somebody else. Very often, people experience both. Yet, few people will admit that they hate somebody; most people will say things like "I can't stand so and so." Once, I heard a prominent KKK member say during an interview, "We don't hate black people, we just want them out of our country." Who can forget the crimes this organization perpetrated against African Americans? Yet, they won't admit being motivated by hate.

On the other hand, many people are quick to point the fingers at those they think don't like them and label them as "haters," "enemies," and even "frenemies."

The Bible has a different take on hatred, a much stronger stance against it.

[15] Whosoever hateth his brother is a murderer: and ye know that no murderer hath eternal life abiding in him. 1 John 3: 15.

God views hatred as murder; therefore, those who hate deserve the same punishment as those who commit murder, death.

[14] We know that we have passed from death unto life, because we love the brethren. He that loveth not his brother abideth in death. 1 John 3: 14.

Hatred is a grievous sin that people, including Christians, often minimize and trifle with. God doesn't want His children to hate anyone regardless of the reason.

To make his point, John went back to the book of Genesis and use the story of the first murder ever committed as an example.

[11] For this is the message that ye heard from the beginning, that we should love one another.

[12] Not as Cain, who was of that wicked one, and slew his brother. And wherefore slew he him? Because his own works were evil, and his brother's righteous. 1 John 3: 11, 12.

The message of love that Jesus brought into this world was there from the beginning. Cain was the first to manifest hate toward someone else, his own brother. As a result of this feeling, he killed him. If you are not familiar with this story, read it in Genesis 4: 1-16. God considers hate and murder the same because before the act of killing takes place, it must be conceived in the heart. Therefore, the 6th commandment, "You shall not murder" may be read, "You shall not hate."

The most painful experience a human being may go through is to love someone that doesn't love him or her in return. One night, while I was working in the Emergency Department at a hospital, the cops brought in a twenty-year old woman. She was escorted to the locked section of the E.D. She was in tears; she seemed anxious, sad, and fearful. Apparently, she swallowed a bunch of pills to end her life. I personally was intrigued by the situation and wanted to know why such a beautiful, young, and healthy woman would do something like that. As she was crying on the phone while talking to someone, she repeatedly said, "he cheated again, he cheated again..." She attempted to commit suicide because her boyfriend was cheating on her. I know some of you may be thinking, "What a dumb thing to do!" "Just move on!" "You can find a better man!" To be honest, these thoughts crossed my mind too; but that was because I didn't understand how painful it was to love someone that didn't love back. How many teenagers attempt suicide every year or do drugs just to get the attention of their parents? How many senior citizens are heartbroken, living in isolation at home or at a nursing home because their children don't care about them?

Even worst, this hurtful experience can cause love to mutate into hate. How many women wish death on their (ex) husband or boyfriend because of the abuse they received from the man they once loved? Some go as far as to murder the man they once could not imagine living their lives without. The pain of rejected love can lead people to do crazy things!

Yet, Jesus expects us to love without expecting love in return. In fact, He wants us to love knowing that our love will be rejected and will even stir hatred in the heart of many.

[13] Marvel not, my brethren, if the world hate you. 1 John 3: 13.

As the men and women of this world sink deeper into sin and unrighteousness, they will hate more and more those who stand for love and righteousness. I will go into more details on how to deal with those who don't love us later in this book.

Chapter 4

Love Demands Sacrifice

Being disconnected from God after eating the forbidden fruit, Adam and Eve were doomed to die. However, God would not let that happened. He had to come up with a way to reconnect Himself with humanity so that His creatures would continue to live. He had two options; first, He could "program" man like a computer, this way people would always be good and righteous; that would have been the easy way. Second, He could demonstrate so much love that man would choose to follow Him. He chose the latter.

[16] For God so loved the world, that he gave his only begotten Son, that whosoever believeth in him should not perish, but have everlasting life.

[17] For God sent not his Son into the world to condemn the world; but that the world through him might be saved.

John 3:16- 17.

The first key to love is sacrifice. God showed His love for you and me by paying the price for our sins, which is death.

For the wages of sin is death; but the gift of God is eternal life through Jesus Christ our Lord. Roman 6: 23.

Let's face the fact, nothing on earth is as horrible as death. Nothing scares us as much as death. That's because God didn't create us to die; it's not part of the cycle of life, unlike some scientists would want us to believe. That's why we can't get used to it; every time we lose someone, we become sad even when the person's death was expected. Life is therefore the biggest gift that can be donated to an individual. Can you think of something bigger?

By giving His life for us, Jesus hoped to demonstrate His love for us and in return, we would show Him love as well.

And I, if I be lifted up from the earth, will draw all men unto me. John 12:32.

By dying on the cross, Jesus took the punishment that we deserved, so that we might have life in abundance. This sacrifice shows to all men and women that God wants to reconnect with them. Humanity broke the connection, God restored it. Therefore, the ministry of Jesus was all about bringing people and God together in harmony.

[18] And all things are of God, who hath reconciled us to himself by Jesus Christ, and hath given to us the ministry of reconciliation;

[19] To wit, that God was in Christ, reconciling the world unto himself, not imputing their trespasses unto them; and hath committed unto us the word of reconciliation.

[20] Now then we are ambassadors for Christ, as though God did beseech you by us: we pray you in Christ's stead, be ye reconciled to God.

²¹ For he hath made him to be sin for us, who knew no sin; that we might be made the righteousness of God in him.

1 Corinthians 5: 18- 21.

One of the most popular quotes attributed to Mahatma Gandhi -there's no proof that he really said it- is this, "I like your Christ. I do not like your Christians. Your Christians are so unlike your Christ." Well, Jesus wants His Christians to be like Him, that is, to love like He loved, sacrificially.

¹⁶ Hereby perceive we the love of God, because he laid down his life for us: and we ought to lay down our lives for the brethren. 1 John 3:16.

Do you understand how serious God is about love? Today the word "love" is used so loosely that it is void of any meaning: A man sees a sexually attractive woman passing by and he is already shouting "I love you." A woman meets a man that is cocky and funny, and she is already "falling in love." In the media and entertainment industry, love is synonymous with sex; "I love you" actually means "I want to have sex with you."

For Christians, saying "I love you" actually means "I am ready to literally die for you if needed just like Christ died for me." It's not for no reason that traditional marriage vows end with "till death do us part." So many couples rather just "move in" together rather than commit themselves knowing that their love is not up to the standard that Christ has set. In our world, many spouses would rather kill their partners than die for them. The man who truly loves his wife is the one who is ready to give his life for her and vice-versa. "Husbands, love your wives, even as Christ also loved the church, and gave himself for it;" Ephesians 5: 25. If as a society, we decide to follow this Godly principle and love our wives sacrificially, we would eradicate rape, divorce, and abuse against women. Men and women are trying so hard to come up with their own solutions to problems that God has already told us how to resolve, and they are failing miserably at achieving that.

The concept of GIVING to those we love is already engrained in us. When a man is interested in a woman, he starts by giving her flowers, paying for her meal at restaurants, and buying her tickets for different types of entertainment. Parents give toys, clothes, education to their children because they love them. Therefore, giving has always been an expression of love and the more someone loves the more he or she gives.

My personal definition of sacrifice is to give beyond what is reasonable. A loving mother would give up her last morsel of bread to her child and go hungry even when she has no hope of obtaining food herself. This may be common sense to you, but according to mainstream science today that shamelessly promotes "survival of the fittest," the normal thing would be for the mother to eat the food and let the baby die.

When someone gives us a cheap gift, while we know he or she can effortlessly give us better, we consider his or her love as cheap as well. We see this as a sign that the giver's feelings toward us are not very strong. On the other hand, when we receive a gift, even a low price and poor quality one that we know is beyond the means of the giver, we interpret it as a sign of great love, sacrificial love. Jesus illustrated this in the story of THE POOR WIDOW:

[41] And Jesus sat over against the treasury, and beheld how the people cast money into the treasury: and many that were rich cast in much.

[42] And there came a certain poor widow, and she threw in two mites, which make a farthing.

[43] And he called unto him his disciples, and saith unto them, Verily I say unto you, That this poor widow hath cast more in, than all they which have cast into the treasury:

[44] For all they did cast in of their abundance; but she of her want did cast in all that she had, even all her living. Mark 12: 41-44.

Even though the amount she gave was less in value than what the other people in the congregation gave, in the eyes of Jesus it was more because she gave sacrificially. Her gift was the expression of the tremendous love she had for God. Beware my friend of preachers who encourage their followers to give large amount of money to their ministries in exchange of great blessings. I have heard- you probably have too- prominent Christian leaders and televangelists promising healing, debt forgiveness, or great wealth to those who would donate above a certain amount. That's WRONG! Although God demands us to be faithful in our tithes and expects us to give generous offerings, for Him it's never about the amount; it's always about the disposition of the heart. God's blessings are not for sale neither are they auctioned. They are gifts; make sure you have a strong relationship with the Giver.

Sacrifice is one of the hallmarks of love. We all have made sacrifices in our lives whether it's for someone in order to obtain something, or to achieve a goal. Therefore, we are familiar with the concept as well as the pain and suffering that come with it. In the end, it's the result that matters. Jesus sets the tone by making the ultimate sacrifice for you and me. In return, He wants us to love Him and the people around us the same way. Would you give it a try?

Chapter 5

Love Requires Action

In romantic movies, when two people say, "I love you," the scene that follows is usually sexual in nature. There are situations where a partner would ask the other one to commit a crime to prove his or her love. These are examples of how love has been perverted in our society. However, there is an important point that I want to make: love is always followed by ACTION. Anybody can claim to love, but it's by his or her actions that people will know whether or not the professed love is real.

[18] My little children, let us not love in word, neither in tongue; but in deed and in truth.

[19] And hereby we know that we are of the truth, and shall assure our hearts before him. 1 John 3: 18, 19.

Jesus sets the example for us; read the accounts of His life. For three and a half year, He went throughout the land of Israel doing good to prove that He loves His people. He healed those who were sick and handicapped. He resurrected many who were dead. He fed those who didn't have food. He even provided financial means to those who couldn't pay their debts. Jesus evaluates love not by how many times people say it, but how much action they take. Consider this parable found in the Gospel according to Matthew:

[31] When the Son of man shall come in his glory, and all the holy angels with him, then shall he sit upon the throne of his glory:

[32] And before him shall be gathered all nations: and he shall separate them one from another, as a shepherd divideth his sheep from the goats:

[33] And he shall set the sheep on his right hand, but the goats on the left.

[34] Then shall the King say unto them on his right hand, Come, ye blessed of my Father, inherit the kingdom prepared for you from the foundation of the world:

[35] For I was an hungred, and ye gave me meat: I was thirsty, and ye gave me drink: I was a stranger, and ye took me in:

[36] Naked, and ye clothed me: I was sick, and ye visited me: I was in prison, and ye came unto me.

[37] Then shall the righteous answer him, saying, Lord, when saw we thee an hungred, and fed thee? or thirsty, and gave thee drink?

[38] When saw we thee a stranger, and took thee in? or naked, and clothed thee?

[39] Or when saw we thee sick, or in prison, and came unto thee?

[40] And the King shall answer and say unto them, Verily I say unto you, Inasmuch as ye have done it unto one of the least of these my brethren, ye have done it unto me.

41 Then shall he say also unto them on the left hand, Depart from me, ye cursed, into everlasting fire, prepared for the devil and his angels:

42 For I was an hungred, and ye gave me no meat: I was thirsty, and ye gave me no drink:

43 I was a stranger, and ye took me not in: naked, and ye clothed me not: sick, and in prison, and ye visited me not.

44 Then shall they also answer him, saying, Lord, when saw we thee an hungred, or athirst, or a stranger, or naked, or sick, or in prison, and did not minister unto thee?

45 Then shall he answer them, saying, Verily I say unto you, Inasmuch as ye did it not to one of the least of these, ye did it not to me.

46 And these shall go away into everlasting punishment: but the righteous into life eternal.

Matthew 25: 31 -46.

In this text, Jesus contrasts the actions of those who are saved vs those who are not. It can be concisely summarized in these words: people who will inherit eternal life are those who care for others, while those who will be lost don't. It is important to clarify that we are not saved by our actions, but by GRACE. There is nothing that you and I can do to deserve eternal life.

[8] For by grace are ye saved through faith; and that not of yourselves: it is the gift of God:

[9] Not of works, lest any man should boast. Ephesians 2: 8-9.

Google Dictionary defines grace as, "The free and unmerited favor of God, as manifested in the salvation of sinners and the bestowal of blessings." In other words, no one deserves salvation; no matter how good you think you are, you will never be good enough for heaven.

²³ For all have sinned, and come short of the glory of God;

²⁴ Being justified freely by his grace through the redemption that is in Christ Jesus: Romans 3: 23, 24.

By dying on the cross, Jesus gives us grace. Those who accept His grace receive eternal life without them having to do anything at all. Remember the thief on the cross who was on the right side of Jesus (Luke 23: 39-43); he committed lots of crimes during his lifetime. But on the cross, he accepted the grace of God. Jesus instantly granted him access to eternal life. The thief on the right died a saved man even though he didn't perform any good work for anybody. He didn't get a chance to go around helping others, yet his salvation was assured at the cross. My friend, you have nothing to do to be saved other than say, "yes" to Jesus and accept His grace regardless of the bad things you did in your life. Would you say "yes" to Him today?

The question you might be asking yourself right now, "If salvation is that simple, why is Jesus stressing out good deeds in the parable above?" When someone is saved, he or she starts to emulate the life of the Savior which was a life of good deeds. Anybody can claim to be saved, but it's in his or her actions that we will know whether he or she is really walking with the Lord, "[20]Wherefore by their fruits ye shall know them." Matthew 7: 20. However, before you start judging other people's actions, start by looking at your own. It's easy to point fingers at others, but you need to live like Christ lived.

One final point in this chapter, Jesus said, "For ye have the poor always with you;…" Matthew 26:11; in other words, regardless of your situation there's always someone that is worse off than you. You may be worried about your rent for the month, but there's someone not far from you living in the street. You may be starving because you couldn't afford lunch today, but in some part of the world people haven't eaten for days. There are people who have plenty of money but are miserable in other aspect of their lives. How many times have we been shocked by news reports about famous and rich people committing suicide? Jesus places the burden upon us to relieve the misery of those around us to the extent that He enables us. The help that we offer them may be in the form of money, counsel, or service; whatever the case, we need to take action on behalf of those who are suffering.

It is important to point out that we do good to others not because they deserve it, but because we love them. Love is what prompts us to help and be a blessing to others. Parents feed and clothe their children because they love them. A husband provides for and respects his wife because he loves her. We help the poor and assist the handicap because we love them. Can you imagine what life would be on earth if everyone decided they would perform good deeds to others every day? Our world is in the state that it is today because the bad things that are performed on a daily outnumbers the good ones.

Nevertheless, let's love and do good to those in our circle of influence, in our neighborhood, in the church, in the prison, as far as we can reach.

Chapter 6

Love is a Principle

We usually define love as a feeling; this is a weak concept although it sounds good. The reason is feelings tend to vary according to circumstances. Consider these two scenarios: 1) You wake up in the morning and the sun is shining. You eat your favorite breakfast that your spouse took the time to prepare for you. All your debts are paid for the month and you have surplus of money in your savings account. Life is good! John Doe comes and asks you for help at that moment, most likely, you will be happy to help. 2) You head to work and your boss screams at you for no apparent reason in front of your peers. This will affect the rest of your day as anger and frustration replace joy and satisfaction. John Doe comes and asks you for help at that time, you will probably reject his appeal. You may even take your anger out on him. Feelings are like the stock market; they go up and down based on circumstances. This is one of the biggest, yet underestimated reasons why so many relationships don't last.

[7] Beloved, let us love one another: for love is of God; and every one that loveth is born of God, and knoweth God. 1 John 4: 7.

John admonishes us to love others, he doesn't mention any circumstances because love is not an option for the Christian, it's an imperative. My favorite author, Ellen G. White, said, "True love is a high and holy principle" (White, 30). A principle is something that doesn't change or vary but stays the same regardless of circumstances. God consistently repeats throughout the Bible that He loves His Creatures even those who don't love Him.

[20] The soul that sinneth, it shall die. The son shall not bear the iniquity of the father, neither shall the father bear the iniquity of the son: the righteousness of the righteous shall be upon him, and the wickedness of the wicked shall be upon him.

Serge Destin

²¹ But if the wicked will turn from all his sins that he hath committed, and keep all my statutes, and do that which is lawful and right, he shall surely live, he shall not die.

²² All his transgressions that he hath committed, they shall not be mentioned unto him: in his righteousness that he hath done he shall live.

²³ Have I any pleasure at all that the wicked should die? saith the Lord God: and not that he should return from his ways, and live? Ezekiel 18: 20- 23.

"God loves sinners but despises sins," that's a popular quote that you are probably familiar with. He wants sinners to turn their lives around not so that He can love them, but because He already loves them. The parable of the PRODIGAL SON is a great and yet simple illustration,

¹¹ And he said, A certain man had two sons:

¹² And the younger of them said to his father, Father, give me the portion of goods that falleth to me. And he divided unto them his living.

¹³ And not many days after the younger son gathered all together, and took his journey into a far country, and there wasted his substance with riotous living.

¹⁴ And when he had spent all, there arose a mighty famine in that land; and he began to be in want.

¹⁵ And he went and joined himself to a citizen of that country; and he sent him into his fields to feed swine.

¹⁶ And he would fain have filled his belly with the husks that the swine did eat: and no man gave unto him.

¹⁷ And when he came to himself, he said, How many hired servants of my father's have bread enough and to spare, and I perish with hunger!

¹⁸ I will arise and go to my father, and will say unto him, Father, I have sinned against heaven, and before thee,

[19] And am no more worthy to be called thy son: make me as one of thy hired servants.

[20] And he arose, and came to his father. But when he was yet a great way off, his father saw him, and had compassion, and ran, and fell on his neck, and kissed him.

[21] And the son said unto him, Father, I have sinned against heaven, and in thy sight, and am no more worthy to be called thy son.

[22] But the father said to his servants, Bring forth the best robe, and put it on him; and put a ring on his hand, and shoes on his feet:

[23] And bring hither the fatted calf, and kill it; and let us eat, and be merry:

[24] For this my son was dead, and is alive again; he was lost, and is found. And they began to be merry.

Luke 18: 11-24.

During the years that the prodigal son spent away wasting his life and goods, the father never stopped loving him. He was waiting anxiously for the son to return and when he finally did, the father held him in his arms, kissed him, restored him, and threw an awesome celebration.

[10] Herein is love, not that we loved God, but that he loved us, and sent his Son to be the propitiation for our sins. 1 John 4: 10.

Love is a principle; it doesn't change even if you and I change. God loves us when we are faithful to Him as well as when we are unfaithful.

[6] For when we were yet without strength, in due time Christ died for the ungodly.

[7] For scarcely for a righteous man will one die: yet peradventure for a good man some would even dare to die.

[8] But God commendeth his love toward us, in that, while we were yet sinners, Christ died for us.

Romans 5: 6-8.

God loves us all the same regardless of our circumstances and lifestyle: rich or poor, black or white, man or woman, Israelite or gentile. There's nothing we can do to keep God from loving us. There's nothing we can say to make Him hate us. Love is a principle, a solid rock that cannot be moved. it cannot be altered, nor changed. It cannot turn into hatred nor bitterness. It is always selfless, never selfish. It is always compassionate, never insensitive. It is always generous, never indifferent. It is always kind, never harsh. It is always patient, never defiant. It endures always and never grows weary. It seeks always the well-being of others, never their destruction.

Chapter 7

God is Love

In 1 John 4: 8, the apostle made one of the boldest declaration in the whole Bible, "He that loveth not knoweth not God; for God is love." Just to make sure his readers don't miss out on this revelation, he repeated it eight verses later, "And we have known and believed the love that God hath to us. God is love; and he that dwelleth in love dwelleth in God, and God in him." 1 John 4: 16. Love is the essence of God: love cannot exist without God. My brother/sister, if you are worshipping a god who is NOT full of love for everyone, you are worshipping a false god. If you are serving a god that only loves people based on DNA, or nationality, or skin color, you are not worshipping the God of the Bible.

But seriously, how many people in this world believe that God is love? God has been held responsible for so many bad things: the flood that wiped out humanity except for Noah and his family, diseases and suffering, famine, death, wars of religions aka the crusades, slavery and racism, not to mention the natural disasters that even atheists referred to as "acts of God" such as earthquakes, tsunamis, and tornados. What a rap sheet!

Answering these objections is not the purpose of this volume, maybe I'll address them in a follow up book if that's what the Lord wants. One point I want to make in this chapter is that all throughout the Bible, God has consistently condemned violence, injustice, oppression which include slavery, theft, and murder. He has boldly called man to stand for and practice justice and equity, to care for the sick, the widows, and orphans, to provide for the needy and set the captives/slaves free. Here are some verses that I would like you to reflect on.

6Is not this the fast that I have chosen? to loose the bands of wickedness, to undo the heavy burdens, and to let the oppressed go free, and that ye break every yoke?

7 Is it not to deal thy bread to the hungry, and that thou bring the poor that are cast out to thy house? when thou

seest the naked, that thou cover him; and that thou hide not thyself from thine own flesh?

[10] And if thou draw out thy soul to the hungry, and satisfy the afflicted soul; then shall thy light rise in obscurity, and thy darkness be as the noon day: Isaiah 58: 6, 7, 10.

[8] He hath shewed thee, O man, what is good; and what doth the Lord require of thee, but to do justly, and to love mercy, and to walk humbly with thy God? Micah 6: 8.

[3] To do justice and judgment is more acceptable to the Lord than sacrifice. Proverbs 21: 3.

[16] These six things doth the Lord hate: yea, seven are an abomination unto him:

[17] A proud look, a lying tongue, and hands that shed innocent blood,

[18] An heart that deviseth wicked imaginations, feet that be swift in running to mischief,

[19] A false witness that speaketh lies, and he that soweth discord among brethren. Proverbs 6: 16- 19.

There are many more verses that testify that God is love and cares for the condition of humankind. Also, you need to consider the many stories of deliverance from oppression, disease, and debt that God operated in favor of His children.

However, the most striking proof of God's tender loving care for all is manifested in the life of Jesus-Christ. If you have not read any of the gospels, I invite you to do so; you can start with any of them. In any case I am sure that you have heard of some of His miracles and stories, at least have seen some of them depicted in the movies portraying His life. Just for your benefit, here is a list of some teachings and actions that Jesus posed while on earth that proves His love for everyone:

- In the Beatitudes, Jesus blessed those who were unfortunate, poor, and suffering. He promised them a better lot in life: Matthew 5: 1- 12.

- Jesus provided for those who were in need and taught His followers to do the same. Matthew 6: 1- 4. Matthew 14: 13- 21. Matthew 15: 29- 38. John 2: 1- 11.

- Jesus relieved the sufferings of others. He cared for the sick and healed many of them. Matthew 8: 1-4, 5-13, 14- 16. Mark 7: 31- 37. Mark 10: 46- 52. Luke 5: 17 – 26.

- Jesus rescued those who were in harms' way: Matthew 8: 23- 27.

- Jesus overcame man's greatest enemy, death, by raising many who had passed away. Matthew 9: 18-23. Luke 6: 11-16. John 11: 38- 43.

- Jesus fought against the prejudice and racism that prevailed in the society He lived in: Matthew 15: 21-28 (The Canaanites were considered inferior to the Jews; Jesus elevated that woman). Luke 5: 27- 31 (The pharisees, the spiritual leaders, didn't mingle with publicans and "sinners." Jesus broke this barrier. He mingled with both groups and threated them the same.) Luke 7: 1- 9 (The Jews and Romans were enemies; yet, Jesus showed sincere appreciation for this Centurion and granted his request.) Luke 10:25- 37 and John 4: 1- 26, 39- 42 (Jesus taught His disciples to stop their discriminations against the Samaritans.)

- Jesus taught and practiced mercy, justice, and forgiveness: Matthew 18: 21- 35. Luke 6: 27- 36. Luke 19: 1- 9. John 8: 1- 11.

All these miracles and teachings were not random acts; they were consistent with the character and mission of Jesus- Christ.

[17] and the scroll of the prophet Isaiah was handed to him. Unrolling it, he found the place where it is written:

[18] "The Spirit of the Lord is on me,

because he has anointed me

to proclaim good news to the poor.

He has sent me to proclaim freedom for the prisoners

and recovery of sight for the blind,

to set the oppressed free,

19   to proclaim the year of the Lord's favor."

20 Then he rolled up the scroll, gave it back to the attendant and sat down. The eyes of everyone in the synagogue were fastened on him. 21 He began by saying to them, "Today this scripture is fulfilled in your hearing." Luke 4: 17- 21 (NIV).

What a marvelous Savior we have!

The disciples continued the work Jesus started and expanded it to the whole world; here are a few examples:

- The disciples provided for the needy: Acts 2: 44- 45. Acts 4: 32- 37; 9: 36- 43.

- They cared for and healed those who were sick: Acts 3: 1- 9; 5: 12- 16; 28: 1-10;

- They overcame prejudice and racism: Acts 8: 4- 8, 26- 40 (Philip preached to Middle-Easterners as well as Africans); Acts 10; 11: 1- 18 (Peter preached to Europeans and taught the other disciples to breakdown the barriers that separated human beings.)

- The disciples raised many who were dead: Acts 20: 7- 12.

It is our turn now to take over the mantle and continue to enlarge the work that Jesus has started. Can you imagine what the world would look like if the so-called 2 billion professed Christians in this world were following in the footsteps of the disciples? Paradise. Unfortunately, we have dropped to ball. To be honest, it is not entirely our fault; the work stopped at the beginning of the 4th Century and Christianity took a turn for the worst. With the arrival of Constantine as Emperor of Rome, the church started to embrace pagans' customs, practices, and beliefs. Christians stopped emulating Christ. They switched their focus to acquiring wealth and power in this world; discrimination, war, crusades, racism, and slavery ensued. Today, Christianity is at a very low point, maybe its lowest ever. You and I need to take our eyes off religion, while remaining religious, and place them on Jesus-Christ. We need to stop looking up to our pastors, ministers, or bishops and follow the example that the Lord left for us.

...

For a concise history of Christianity since the days of the apostles to modern day churches, I suggest you read THE GREAT CONTROVERSY by ELLEN G. WHITE

Chapter 8

Love made Perfect

I have been writing about love since the beginning of this book and yet, I have not defined the word LOVE itself and I don't intend to. Many authors, speakers, artists, along with some of the most brilliant minds who walked this earth through the centuries have attempted to define it, but they always fell short because they did so based on its manifestations. For instance, it's no secret, there are different degrees in love. Teachers tend to show more love and care to the A+ well-behaved students than the D- troublemaking ones; you probably love your friends more than your colleagues. In addition, there are different types of love. The love you have for your parents is different from the love you have for your favorite celebrity. The love a husband has for his wife is very unique, only she can understand and experience it, so also a wife can never love another man the same way she loves her husband.

Love is so complex that it can only be of a divine origin, evolutionary scientists can't and will never be able to explain it. GOD IS LOVE (1 john 4: 8, 16). No one can explain God nor perfectly understand Him. In case that sounds mythical to you, let me remind you that we don't understand our own species either. Let's not fool ourselves by trying to figure out the nature of God; the fact that we can't comprehend Him doesn't mean He doesn't exist nor that we cannot have a close relationship with Him. We form close bond with our spouse and children, yet we barely know who they are, as they most of the time do things we never thought they could have done, right? However, there is something important that God wants you and I to grasp, HIS CHARACTER.

When Moses wanted to see God, this is what He said,

[18] And he said, I beseech thee, shew me thy glory.

[19] And he said, I will make all my goodness pass before thee, and I will proclaim the name of the Lord before

thee; and will be gracious to whom I will be gracious, and will shew mercy on whom I will shew mercy.

20 And he said, Thou canst not see my face: for there shall no man see me, and live. Exodus 33: 18- 20.

4 And he hewed two tables of stone like unto the first; and Moses rose up early in the morning, and went up unto mount Sinai, as the Lord had commanded him, and took in his hand the two tables of stone.

5 And the Lord descended in the cloud, and stood with him there, and proclaimed the name of the Lord.

6 And the Lord passed by before him, and proclaimed, The Lord, The Lord God, merciful and gracious, longsuffering, and abundant in goodness and truth,

7 Keeping mercy for thousands, forgiving iniquity and transgression and sin, and that will by no means clear the guilty; visiting the iniquity of the fathers upon the children, and upon the children's children, unto the third and to the fourth generation. Exodus 34: 4- 7.

God is not interested in showing to humans what He looks like, His size, His skin, or His power. It amazes me to see how much time and energy people spent trying to figure out Jesus' skin color, His race, his type of beard and hair, and His genetic code. If you care about these characteristics, you are missing the point of Jesus' mission. What He wants you to focus on is His character which is exactly the same as His Father's. He wants humanity to understand that He is good, gracious, merciful, longsuffering, that is patient, truthful, honest, always willing to forgive and yet just. All these are different aspect of love. When my kids are doing something bad, I tell them to stop. Sometimes, they don't listen and continue to do it. So, I have to repeat myself 3 or 4 times; that's patience. Then I have to punish them for their wrongdoing; that's justice. After a few minutes, they come crawling into my arms saying they are sorry, and I forgive them; by the way, I forgave them before they were punished, but they didn't know about it. I do these things because I love them. Everything that God does is motivated by love and is for the benefit of the human race. I know there are some stories in the Bible where God made some harsh decisions that APPEAR to be unfair, but if you take the time to understand the circumstances, you will find out that they are totally justified. In the end, God wants to save us and to offer us a better life because He loves us. He loves every single individual born on this earth regardless of his or her race, nationality, social rank, or financial status. Love is the essence of God. GOD IS LOVE.

"So God created man in his OWN IMAGE, in the IMAGE OF GOD created he him; male and female created he them." Genesis 1: 27 (emphasis added). Love was instilled in us at creation; it's woven in every cell of our body. However, the level of love that God created humanity with has decreased drastically because of sin. As a matter of fact, there's barely anything left today, "And because iniquity shall abound, the love of many shall wax cold." Matthew 24: 12. So sin is inversely proportional to love, the more sin the less love. Think about it, the more a person cheats on his or her spouse, which is the sin of adultery, the less he or she will love the partner which might result in a divorce.

This can be seen in the story of our first parents. In Genesis 2: 23, Adam was happy to see Eve, "And Adam said, this is now bone of my bones, and flesh of my flesh: she shall be called Woman, because she was taken out of Man." He loved her as he loved himself because she was a part of him, she completed him. However, after they sinned, he talked about Eve like she was a curse, "And the man said, the woman whom thou gavest to be with me, she gave me of the tree, and I did eat." Genesis 3: 12. You can spot in his language that he didn't love her the same way as before. His love for her decreased, and I bet her feelings for him decreased as well. Ever since, sin has been increasing in this world: Cain envied Abel, he became jealous, headstrong, and disobedient. Hatred grew in his heart and he stopped loving his brother. Then one day, he killed him; yet he felt no remorse. Sin

Serge Destin

has overtaken the world today, this is why there's only a little bit of love left.

God calls us to bring love back to counter the power of sin in our midst; this is our mission.

18 And Jesus came and spake unto them, saying, All power is given unto me in heaven and in earth.

19 Go ye therefore, and teach all nations, baptizing them in the name of the Father, and of the Son, and of the Holy Ghost:

20 Teaching them to observe all things whatsoever I have COMMANDED you: and, lo, I am with you always, even unto the end of the world. Amen. Matthew 28: 18-20. (emphasis added)

The gospel, which means "good news," is about teaching others what Jesus commanded us. And what did Jesus command us?

21 And this commandment have we from him, That he who loveth God love his brother also. 1 John 4: 21.

But first, the love that we have in our heart needs to grow and reach a new level.

Chapter 9

Next level of love

"Love those who love you and forget those who don't value you."

"You want to make your life beautiful, start loving those who love you and ignore anyone else."

"Spend your time on those that love you unconditionally. Don't waste it on those that only love you when the conditions are right for them."

People tend to love these types of quotes. I don't' know who their authors are, but they are quite popular on social media. Even Christian ministers love to repeat them; that's so unfortunate. This is what I call the WISDOM OF THE WORLD. Although they sound wise, they represent love at its lowest level. When someone is good to you, it is expected that you will love that person in return. In the same way, if you take good care of your dog, he or she will love you. That's basic instinct.

Jesus addressed this issue in the sermon on the mount.

[43] Ye have heard that it hath been said, Thou shalt love thy neighbour, and hate thine enemy.

[44] But I say unto you, Love your enemies, bless them that curse you, do good to them that hate you, and pray for them which despitefully use you, and persecute you;

[45] That ye may be the children of your Father which is in heaven: for he maketh his sun to rise on the evil and on the good, and sendeth rain on the just and on the unjust.

[46] For if ye love them which love you, what reward have ye? do not even the publicans the same?

[47] And if ye salute your brethren only, what do ye more than others? do not even the publicans so?

[48] Be ye therefore perfect, even as your Father which is in heaven is perfect. Matthew 5: 43- 48.

This is the next level, better yet, the ultimate level of love. Jesus set the example for us on the cross. His death is the worst case of injustice ever perpetrated on earth. Jesus was a public figure known by all living in Israel at that time for His goodness, compassion, fairness, wisdom, charity, no-nonsense teachings, and power to perform miracles. Despite this display of love, He was - and still is- the most hated man in the world. He was doing so much good that the forces of darkness couldn't bear Him for more than three and a half years. The religious leaders joined forces with the military might of the Roman empire to kill Him. Jesus was arrested without any charge brought against Him; He was accused of no crimes. He was tried seven times without representation in less than 24 hours by different tribunals under both Jewish and Roman laws. He was found innocent at every trial, yet still got the death penalty. All throughout this process, He was mocked, beaten, tortured, humiliated, disgraced, dragged around like an animal, like a lamb being led to the butcher. Hate, sin, and evil were in full display; mankind had reached the bottom of moral degradation. Humanity showed its worst character at the foot of the cross. Yet, even while going through His greatest pain, Jesus looked on the multitude with pity and interceded on their behalf, "Father, forgive them; for they know not what they do" Luke 23: 34. There was no trace of hate in the heart of Jesus; His love for the fallen race didn't diminish at all. There's nothing we can do to make Jesus hate us. God cannot stop loving His creatures; it's impossible.

Jesus calls us to follow in His footsteps. We must reach a level of love where it is impossible for us to hate others regardless of what they do to us. Nobody can treat you and I worse than the way the religious leaders and the Romans treated Jesus. We cannot suffer more than what Jesus suffered for us. We are called to display the same level of love amid our own trials and persecutions.

Stephen, the deacon, was the first Christian martyr. This was his reaction when he was being killed.

[57] Then they cried out with a loud voice, and stopped their ears, and ran upon him with one accord,

⁵⁸ And cast him out of the city, and stoned him: and the witnesses laid down their clothes at a young man's feet, whose name was Saul.

⁵⁹ And they stoned Stephen, calling upon God, and saying, Lord Jesus, receive my spirit.

⁶⁰ And he kneeled down, and cried with a loud voice, Lord, lay not this sin to their charge. And when he had said this, he fell asleep. Acts 7: 57- 60.

Stephen was also a victim of an unfair trial; he was put to death although found innocent. As a matter of fact, he was executed before the trial was over. However, He prayed for those who were throwing stones at him. The purpose of his prayer, just like Jesus' prayer on the cross, was for these evildoers to recognize their wrongdoings, change, and be saved.

This is the level of love we need to reach; this is perfect love.

I enjoy reading, talking, preaching, and writing about the love of Jesus. However, I am nowhere close to reaching that level of love. I am still struggling, but that's the goal I am striving for. So, I'll share with you one of my personal experiences dealing with a friend who hurt me.

After I graduated from nursing and was still preparing to take my board exam, I found a little job working with special needs children to make a little money in the meantime. A friend of mine came to apply at the same job a couple of months later; to be honest we weren't that close, but we hang out together a few times in the past. When my boss found out that I knew her, he asked me if I would recommend her for the job. Without any hesitation I said "yes;" I was very sincere in my answer because I admired her many qualities. Soon after she started the job, she began launching attacks on many co-workers including myself. She was constantly feuding with the staff and managers. Nonetheless, I made a point not to answer to her provocations and endured her mistreatments. However, I prayed for her every day. I asked God to change her heart and open her eyes to see the wrong she was doing. For months, her bad behavior continued and even got worse, I prayed even more. Finally, I decided to have a little talk with her. I prayed about it, then I reached out to her. We put the issues on the table and discussed them. However, at the end of our conversation, I didn't think that she was ready to change although she admitted that her behavior was toxic to the workplace. I continued to pray. She resumed her bad attitude the next day and three days later, she was fired. Peace returned in the facility; I was offered a promotion which I turned down to pursue my career in nursing. We are still friend just like before. Here are five lessons I learned from this experience:

1- **Don't wish evil on anybody:** Sometimes people's behaviors are a way of expressing their own griefs. Their situations may be worse than ours. It's better to find out why they are acting badly.

Once the underlying cause is discovered, we can try to solve the issue.

2- **Keep our tongue under control:** I don't ask anybody to suffer quietly like I did; I would have been justified to get back at her like many of my co-workers were doing. There are many instances where I spoke up to stop unfair treatments. In all cases, wisdom is required. Don't react based on impulse; in her case I thought it was wiser to keep my mouth shut.

[5] Even so the tongue is a little member, and boasteth great things. Behold, how great a matter a little fire kindleth!

[6] And the tongue is a fire, a world of iniquity: so is the tongue among our members, that it defileth the whole body, and setteth on fire the course of nature; and it is set on fire of hell.

[7] For every kind of beasts, and of birds, and of serpents, and of things in the sea, is tamed, and hath been tamed of mankind:

[8] But the tongue can no man tame; it is an unruly evil, full of deadly poison.

[9] Therewith bless we God, even the Father; and therewith curse we men, which are made after the similitude of God.

[10] Out of the same mouth proceedeth blessing and cursing. My brethren, these things ought not so to be. James 3: 5- 10.

3- **Praying for our enemy to change will not necessarily change the person:** When we pray for others, the Holy Spirit will work in their heart to help them recognize their wrongdoings. However, God will not force the person to change; He will help the person to turn around when the person decides to. As a result of Jesus' prayer on the cross, many of the pharisees who were present at His execution including Nicodemus believed in Him. Stephen's prayer touched at least one soul in the crowd, one who will become a pillar in the Christian church, Saul who will be known after his conversion as apostle Paul.

4- **Talk to the person:** [15] Moreover if thy brother shall trespass against thee, go and tell him his fault between thee and him alone: if he shall hear thee, thou hast gained thy brother.

[16] But if he will not hear thee, then take with thee one or two more, that in the mouth of two or three witnesses every word may be established. [17] And if he shall neglect to hear them, tell it unto the church: but if he neglect to hear the church, let him be unto thee as an heathen man and a publican. Matthew 18: 15- 17.

Jesus gave us specific instructions on how to handle someone who offends us whether or not it's done on purpose. First, we need to address the issue with the offender one-on-one in order to resolve it. If the two of us can't solve it, we need to meet again with two or three people to help us come to an agreement. If that fails, then we are free to go to the authorities. This is one of the most ignored counsels given by the Lord even by Christians. When someone does us wrong, our first tendency is to call our friends to report how badly we were treated, sometimes with exaggerations. These confidents in turn recount the story to other people and create a scandal. Then the issue becomes harder to resolve as anger, resentment, and hate build up in the heart of both parties.

5- **Believe that God will deliver:** Deliverance doesn't usually happen at the time and in the way we expect, but God always comes through. Hang on to these texts:

⁶ This poor man cried, and the Lord heard him, and saved him out of all his troubles.

[7] The angel of the Lord encampeth round about them that fear him, and delivereth them.

Psalms 34: 6- 7.

[18] The Lord is nigh unto them that are of a broken heart; and saveth such as be of a contrite spirit.

[19] Many are the afflictions of the righteous: but the Lord delivereth him out of them all. Psalms 34: 18-19.

[11] For I know the thoughts that I think toward you, saith the Lord, thoughts of peace, and not of evil, to give you an expected end. Jeremiah 29: 11.

Let's rise above the popular wisdom of this world and take our love for others to the next level. We will not be able to do that on our own...

Chapter 10

Dwelling in Christ

[12] No man hath seen God at any time. If we love one another, God dwelleth in us, and his love is perfected in us.

[13] Hereby know we that we dwell in him, and he in us, because he hath given us of his Spirit.

[14] And we have seen and do testify that the Father sent the Son to be the Saviour of the world.

[15] Whosoever shall confess that Jesus is the Son of God, God dwelleth in him, and he in God.

[16] And we have known and believed the love that God hath to us. God is love; and he that dwelleth in love dwelleth in God, and God in him. 1 John 4: 12- 16.

In the verses above, the apostle explains to us that reaching perfect love cannot come from us, but only from God. Furthermore, it is sustained by God and will last as long as we maintain our relationship with the Creator. Let me remind you here that God is always trying to have a strong relationship with His creatures; God never initiates breakups. As long as you and I want to be with Him, He is ready to accept us no matter what we did in the past or how messed up we are. We, humans, have the ability to break away from Him.

With all these said, let me share with you 3 basic elements on how to dwell in God:

1- Prayer

Ellen G. White defines prayer as, "opening of the heart to God as to a friend" (Steps to Christ p. 93) The foundation of every good relationship is communication. The great heroes of faith lived a life of prayer. They talked to God at every occasion.

When Eliezer, Abraham's trusted servant, had to pick a wife for his master's son, he prayed and asked God to appoint a young lady to be the spouse of Isaac. Genesis 24: 12- 14.

When Israel sinned, Moses prayed and pleaded with God to forgive them. Exodus 32: 31- 33.

When Hannah wanted a son, she went to the house of the Lord to pray. 1 Samuel 1: 11- 12.

When Solomon built the temple in Jerusalem, he asked God to bless everyone who would come to worship Him in this place. 1 Kings 8: 14- 53.

When the Medo-Persians threatened to exterminate the Jews living in their empire, Queen Esther ordered 3 days of fasting. Esther 4: 15- 16.

When King Hezekiah was on his death bed, he prayed to God for healing. 2 Kings 20: 2- 3.

You need to talk to God multiple times throughout your day. He is always ready to listen to you. You can talk to Him about everything that is weighing on your mind. You need to be vulnerable with Him; after all you cannot hide anything from Him. So, talk to Him: tell Him about the difficulties you are having at work or at school, tell Him about the debts that you have to pay; tell Him to guide you in the choice of a life or business partner; request blessings on your spouse and children; ask Him to heal your pain and illness; ask Him to mend your broken heart.

Jesus lived a life of prayer (Matthew 26: 36- 41; John 17; Matthew 14: 23; Matthew 19: 13; Marc 1: 35; Luke 6: 12). Apostle Paul invites us to do the same, "Pray without ceasing." 1 Thessalonians 5: 17.

2- Study the Bible

Effective communication implies two equally important elements: speaking and listening. If praying is speaking to God, studying the Word is the listening part since the Holy Scriptures is the main method God uses to communicate with us today. He still uses dreams, visions, signs, and prophecies but rarely because His expressed will is already revealed in the Bible for the most part. In order to understand His message, you must be willing to:

- Learn: The books of the Bible weren't written to satisfy our curiosity. Often, we Christians get caught up in intellectual debates that are irrelevant to our salvation. We don't study the Word to justify our belief system, but to comprehend the love of the Father, to understand the sacrifice of the Son, and to know the path to salvation.

- Change: Let me share with you a little secret, SIN MAKES US FEEL GOOD that's why we keep on doing the same sin over and over. We all have our favorite sin: cheating, gossiping, stealing and so forth. Think about how you feel when you are doing it, you experience a pleasant sensation even if sometimes you feel bad after the deed, don't you? The Bible points out OUR sins and weaknesses -not those of somebody else- and bids us to change. Unfortunately, most people are very comfortable in their way of life and don't feel the necessity to change. Hence, the reason why a lot of people don't read the Bible; they don't want to feel bad about their wrongdoings. As I study the Word, I realize that following Its teachings can only make me a better person. I must admit that change is difficult; but when it comes from God, it's always for my benefit. Are you willing to make changes that will better your life?

• Apply: Being a Christian is not a theory neither a one-day a week gig. I know many individuals, including ministers, who speak and act like the devil and yet profess to be believers. They are the main reason why Christianity has a bad name and turns many people off. How can someone be a Christian and support slavery, racial discriminations, wars, oppression of the poor and so forth? We must be Christians every day and strive to apply what we learn from the Word in our lives. We will not be able to do everything at once, but gradually we will improve.

3- Share the Gospel

Most people view sharing the gospel as an inconvenience, an option, or the church leaders' job. Let me tell you, friend, sharing the gospel is an ACT OF LOVE. Love is what motivates you to tell someone about Jesus, salvation, and paradise- a place where he or she will suffer no more, "[4] And God shall wipe away all tears from their eyes; and there shall be no more death, neither sorrow, nor crying, neither shall there be any more pain: for the former things are passed away." Revelation 21: 4. Therefore, it is every believer's responsibility. You may choose different forms of ministry or even create your own type under the guidance of the Holy Spirit, but there are 2 fundamental elements that must be incorporated in it.

1) Teach others about Jesus and instruct them in the Word: That should be obvious, right? Unfortunately, many preachers today have become "motivational speakers," they pick and choose from the Bible only teachings that make their audience "feel good" or that prepare them to live their "best life here and now." There's nothing wrong with teaching others how to have an amazing and fulfilling life on earth, but you must remember as you spread the Word that everything you have now is temporary. You must keep your eyes on eternity, which means that you must share the uncomfortable and unpopular messages that are in the Bible as well. So, find your way of sharing the gospel; it could be one on one, behind a pulpit, through writing books such as this one, or distributing tracks.

2) Care for the needy: Caring for the sick, orphans, widows, poor, and afflicted was a priority for

Jesus and the disciples. Let me remind you of this parable again.

[31] When the Son of man shall come in his glory, and all the holy angels with him, then shall he sit upon the throne of his glory:

[32] And before him shall be gathered all nations: and he shall separate them one from another, as a shepherd divideth his sheep from the goats:

[33] And he shall set the sheep on his right hand, but the goats on the left.

[34] Then shall the King say unto them on his right hand, Come, ye blessed of my Father, inherit the kingdom prepared for you from the foundation of the world:

[35] For I was an hungred, and ye gave me meat: I was thirsty, and ye gave me drink: I was a stranger, and ye took me in:

[36] Naked, and ye clothed me: I was sick, and ye visited me: I was in prison, and ye came unto me.

³⁷ Then shall the righteous answer him, saying, Lord, when saw we thee an hungred, and fed thee? or thirsty, and gave thee drink?

³⁸ When saw we thee a stranger, and took thee in? or naked, and clothed thee?

³⁹ Or when saw we thee sick, or in prison, and came unto thee?

⁴⁰ And the King shall answer and say unto them, Verily I say unto you, Inasmuch as ye have done it unto one of the least of these my brethren, ye have done it unto me. Matthew 25: 31- 40.

These two aspects of sharing the gospel work together; you cannot practice one without the other. On one hand, if you help only and don't tell those in need about Jesus, you don't have a ministry; you have a nonprofit social service. You are helping people live a better life on earth knowing full well that they will miss out on eternity. On the other hand, if you only preach and don't perform any good deeds, this is what Jesus said will happen to you.

⁴¹ Then shall he say also unto them on the left hand, Depart from me, ye cursed, into everlasting fire, prepared for the devil and his angels:

⁴² For I was an hungred, and ye gave me no meat: I was thirsty, and ye gave me no drink:

⁴³ I was a stranger, and ye took me not in: naked, and ye clothed me not: sick, and in prison, and ye visited me not.

⁴⁴ Then shall they also answer him, saying, Lord, when saw we thee an hungred, or athirst, or a stranger, or naked, or sick, or in prison, and did not minister unto thee?

⁴⁵ Then shall he answer them, saying, Verily I say unto you, inasmuch as ye did it not to one of the least of these, ye did it not to me.

[46] And these shall go away into everlasting punishment: but the righteous into life eternal.

Matthew 25: 41- 46.

Ask God how you can best minister to others on His behalf.

Conclusion

[48] Be ye therefore perfect, even as your Father which is in heaven is perfect. Matthew 5: 43- 48.

While reading the book of 1 John, I realized that I am called to become the perfect replica of Jesus Christ, meaning to have perfect love in my heart. The many concepts of love in this world leave room within me for sin, indifference, and hate. Love, as God intended, needs to fill me completely. This is a feat that I cannot achieve on my own. So, I pray God to help me grow the kind of love that He desires for me to have. It's going to take time and trials, but I believe that the Holy Spirit is working in my heart.

[13] Hereby know we that we dwell in him, and he in us, because he hath given us of his Spirit. 1 John 4: 13.

Now, it's your turn to decide what kind of love will be manifested in your life. God is willing to transform you so that everywhere you go others can see in you a source of LOVE.

MAY GOD BLESS YOU.

Serge Destin

What are the points that caught your attention while reading this book?

_____

_____

_____

_____

_____

_____

_____

_____

_____

_____

_____

_____

_____

_____

_____

_____

_____

What can you do to alleviate the suffering of those around you?

Describe your plan of action

_____

_____

_____

_____

_____

_____

_____

_____

_____

_____

_____

_____

_____

_____

Serge Destin

_____

_____

_____

_____

_____

_____

_____

_____

_____

_____

_____

_____

_____

_____

_____

_____

_____

May God be with you as you execute this plan.

References

White, Ellen G. Letters to Young Lovers,

https://m.egwwritings.org/en/book/40.147#147

White, Ellen G. Steps to Christ,

https://m.egwwritings.org/en/book/108/toc

Detroit: Two Bystanders Shot After Argument Over Kool-Aid

https://www.youtube.com/watch?v=YTiAmLmZxGY&t=34s

Merriam-Webster Dictionary

Google Dictionary

Wikipedia. Bernie Madoff. n.d.

https://en.wikipedia.org/wiki/Bernie_Madoff

All biblical references have been taken from the King James Version except otherwise specified.